TESSA THOMPSON

DWAYNE HICKS

PowerKiDS
press.™

New York

Published in 2022 by The Rosen Publishing Group, Inc.
29 East 21st Street, New York, NY 10010

First Edition

Editor: Greg Roza
Cover Design: Michael Flynn
Interior Layout: Rachel Rising

Photo Credits: Cover, p. 1 Frazer Harrison/Staff/Getty Images Entertainment/Getty Images; pp. 4, 6, 8, 10, 12, 14, 16, 18, 20, 21 Woskresenskiy/shutterstock.com; pp. 4, 6, 8, 10, 12, 14, 16, 18, 20, 21 Sunward Art/shutterstock.com; p. 5 Matt Winkelmeyer/Staff/Getty Images Entertainment/Getty Images; p. 7 Scott Gries/Staff/Getty Images Entertainment/Getty Images; p. 9 Amanda Edwards/Contributor/WireImage/Getty Images; p. 11 Getty Images/Stringer/Getty Images Entertainment/Getty Images; p. 13 Albert L. Ortega/Contributor/Getty Images Entertainment/Getty Images; p. 15 J. Merritt/Contributor/Getty Images Entertainment/Getty Images; p. 17 George Pimentel/Contributor/WireImage/Getty Images; p. 19 Todd Williamson/Contributor/Getty Images Entertainment/Getty Images; p. 20 ANTHONY HARVEY/Contributor/AFP/Getty Images.

Library of Congress Cataloging-in-Publication Data

Names: Hicks, Dwayne, author.
Title: Tessa Thompson / Dwayne Hicks.
Description: New York : PowerKids Press, [2022] | Series: African American superstars | Includes index.
Identifiers: LCCN 2020036569 | ISBN 9781725326156 (library binding) | ISBN 9781725326132 (paperback) | ISBN 9781725326149 (6 pack)
Subjects: LCSH: Thompson, Tessa, 1983–Juvenile literature. | African American actresses–Biography–Juvenile literature.
Classification: LCC PN2287.T457 H53 2022 | DDC 791.4302/8092 [B]–dc23
LC record available at https://lccn.loc.gov/2020036569

Manufactured in the United States of America

Find us on

CONTENTS

Meet Tessa!

Tessa Thompson is an actor. She's been in many TV shows and movies. She's also a singer and songwriter. Tessa strongly believes in **diversity**. She works hard to spread this belief to others. Her fans love her for it!

Diverse Family

Tessa Lynne Thompson was born on October 3, 1983, in Los Angeles, California. Tessa has a diverse family. Her father is Black and **Panamanian**. He's also a very good musician. Tessa's mother is English and Mexican.

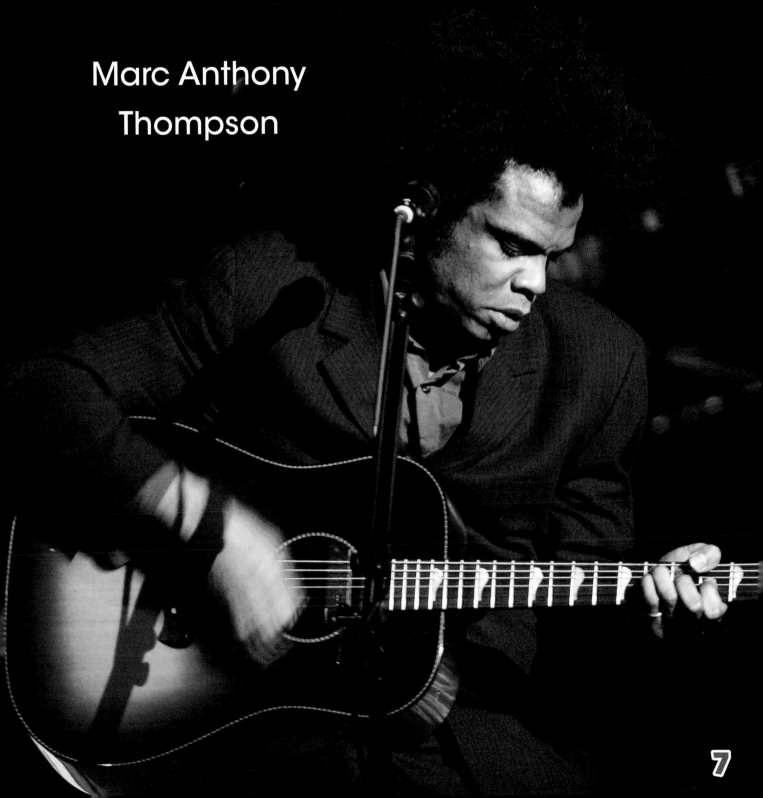

Marc Anthony Thompson

7

In High School

Tessa went to school in Santa Monica, California. She helped form a diversity club in high school. The club brought people from different backgrounds together. She also appeared in plays. She acted in the Shakespeare play *A Midsummer Night's Dream*.

College Years

Tessa started college in 2001. She went to Santa Monica College in California. She learned even more about diversity. Tessa also acted in college plays. She was in another Shakespeare play called *The Tempest*.

TV Success

Tessa has acted in more than 20 TV shows. Her first **role** was on the show *Cold Case*. She appeared in the shows *Veronica Mars* and *Grey's Anatomy*. Tessa also has a large role in the TV show *Westworld.*

 Tessa Thompson

13

Singing Success

In 2014, Tessa was in a band called Caught a Ghost. She wrote music and sang. In 2014, Tessa acted in the movie *Dear White People*. This movie also has two songs from Caught a Ghost.

Award Winner

Tessa won some **awards** for her early movies. She won awards for her roles in the movies *For Colored Girls*, *Dear White People*, and *Selma*. In 2015 and 2016, she won awards for her role in the movie *Creed*.

Action Hits

Tessa has acted in action movies. In 2017, she played a superhero in the movie *Thor: Ragnarok*. In 2019, she played this superhero again in the movie *Avengers: Endgame*. That same year, Tessa appeared in *Men in Black: International*.

Diversity in Movie Making

Most big-movie **directors** are men. Tessa thinks that's unfair. She wants more female directors making movies. She has asked movie **studios** and actors to work with more women directors. Tessa works hard to get more diversity in movies.

TIMELINE

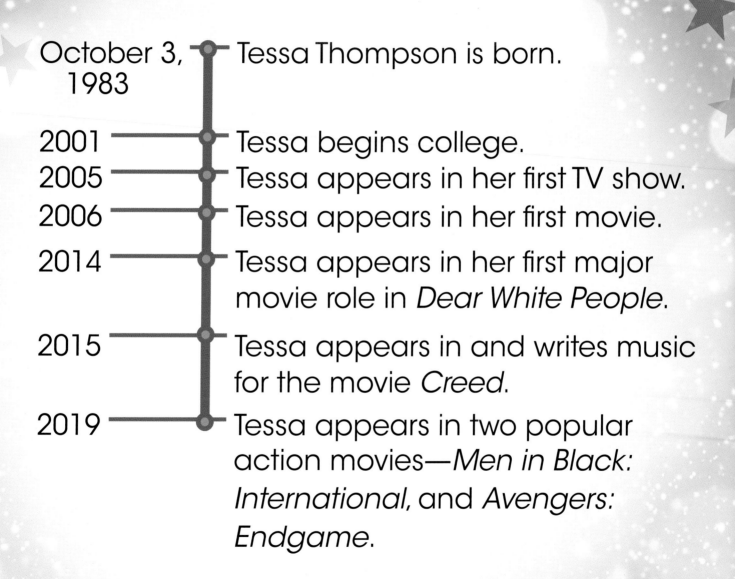

October 3, 1983	Tessa Thompson is born.
2001	Tessa begins college.
2005	Tessa appears in her first TV show.
2006	Tessa appears in her first movie.
2014	Tessa appears in her first major movie role in *Dear White People*.
2015	Tessa appears in and writes music for the movie *Creed*.
2019	Tessa appears in two popular action movies—*Men in Black: International*, and *Avengers: Endgame*.

GLOSSARY

award: Something given to someone for being excellent at what they do.

director: The person in charge of making a movie.

diversity: Having to do with people of different backgrounds.

Panamanian: From the Central American country of Panama.

role: The part played by an actor.

studio: A business that makes movies.

FOR MORE INFORMATION

BOOKS

Bobowicz, Pamela. *What Makes a Hero.* New York, NY: Marvel Press, 2019.

Fitzpatrick, Lisa, and Sharon Gosling. *Men in Black: The Extraordinary Visual Companion to the Films.* London, UK: Titan Books, 2019.

WEBSITES

Tessa Thompson Biography
www.biography.com/actor/tessa-thompson
Learn more about Tessa Thompson on this in-depth site.

Valkyrie
www.marvel.com/characters/valkyrie
Find out more about the character Tessa Thompson plays in the Marvel movies.

Publisher's note to parents and teachers: Our editors have reviewed the websites listed here to make sure they're suitable for students. However, websites may change frequently. Please note that students should always be supervised when they access the internet.

INDEX